The Women of the Bible

Nelfa Chevalier

Visited by the Angel

Gabriel

Mary and Elizabeth

Table of Contents

The Women of the Bible

General Prologue

The Women of the Bible is a collection of biblical books that expose the lives of women mentioned in the Holy Scriptures. The verses quoted in each text were taken, literally, from the Holy Bible. This sacred text is a source of faith, love and peace for Christians who wish to quench their spiritual thirst. His sublime knowledge is life and salvation to our souls. Starting from the concepts exposed in this book about numerous women of past times, we take the most relevant facts of their lives. We begin with valuable stories of Old Testament women, which are intimately linked to the major patriarchs, prophets, and evangelists of that time. Meanwhile, the New Testament presents us with the importance of the female sex, before and during the life of the Messiah, our Lord Jesus Christ.

In an antagonistic way, this same religious work, the Holy Bible, teaches some prototypes of women involved in actions condemned by the laws of our Lord God. In fact, all of them left us significant legacies; some of good and others of evil. The good ones help us grow spiritually, and the bad ones encourage us to change our bad behavior. Therefore, we could draw from the fruits generated by women of values, ladies consecrated to faith in our Lord, the eternal Father. But also, to consider the thorns that sprouted from wicked women, so as not to make the same mistakes as them. Instead, we are to act according to the commandments of our Lord Jesus Christ: to love the Lord and our neighbor.

Let us take advantage of the greatness of spirit that we all have, and let us take the teachings that emanate from the different biblical texts and adapt them in a particular way to our lives. Let us recognize our gifts; but also, our vulnerabilities. In fact, on the basis of this concept, the writer declares the following: physically, the female sex has always been weaker than the male. Spiritually, however, women are firmer and stronger than men. From its creation, this being was endowed with sensitivity and delicacy. In addition, women belong to the life-creating gender. Without woman, nothing that has been created would pre-exist. Only nature would exist.

The goal of this book is to convey messages of faith, love, generosity, humility and unity, which are compatible for all women in the world. It is urgent to achieve this through the admirable and praised examples of countless women who are the protagonists of profuse Bible verses. Building on the commendable performances of virtuous ladies of the Old and New Testaments, who showed absolute faith in God, women today could take them as an example by leading our lives in a dignified, righteous and godly manner. By looking at it that way, we would build homes on rocks that nothing and no one could corrupt or destroy. Their strength would be based on religious foundations where their foundations would be love of God, family and neighbor in general. Thus fulfilling the two great commandments of Christ Jesus:

"To love God above all things and our neighbor as ourselves."

(Matthew 22:36-39).

On that Christian platform there is no evil, but an abundance of good. Since we all pursue the good for our families; We already know how to achieve it, and how far we can lead it to achieve it.

Based on all of the above, all members of the female sex should support and help each other at all times, to work for the causes of our Father God. A helping hand, in times of sadness. Sound advice, if we are deviated or disoriented. Our unconditional help in times of storms. That means being empathetic to our siblings. The fellowship between us fills our heavenly Father with joy, and makes us his true children. Following this line of faith marked by a Christian logistics established by the women presented in the Holy Bible, the book of Genesis cites the first female creation. Her name was Eve, who has been a controversial figure because of her disobedience to God (Genesis 1:27-28; 2:16-17; 3:1-6. 16. 19. 22). Despite her misbehavior, we could all learn from Eve by taking control of ourselves. Certainly, by mastering our evil desires and carnal instincts, we act in the right way by corresponding to the laws of our Creator, God the Father.

Below are extensive sketches of other women who participate in this Christian collection. Starting with Sarah, who is considered one of the great biblical women. Sarah was the wife of the patriarch Abraham. Unfortunately, Sarah could not bear children, and her barrenness was an injury to Abraham who desired to have offspring. Despite her misfortune, Sarah never stopped feeling great faith in God. Therefore, He granted her motherhood at the age of 90, giving birth to her son Isaac, who later became the second patriarch of

Israel (Genesis 15:1-6; 16:1-16; 17:15-27; 18:12; 20:1-7. 12. Verses 14-17).

In another context we place the story of Hannah, mother of the prophet Samuel. Anne's story is analogous to Sarah's, in the aspect of infertility. Like Sarah, Hannah was also barren; but both conceived by the mercy of our holy Father. Although there is a difference between Sara and Ana. According to the Holy Scriptures, God granted Sarah the gift of motherhood in her old age. Meanwhile, the Lord conferred pregnancy on Anne during her youth. Hannah was Jewish and had full faith in God. She was an admirable believer. She became pregnant with her son Samuel, who grew up to become a great prophet (1 Samuel 1:1-28; 2:1-21; 3:19-21).

We continue with the two wives of the patriarch Jacob: Leah and Rachel. Leah was Jacob's first wife. But the one Jacob wanted to marry was Rachel, Leah's younger sister. However, Jewish tradition dictated that the eldest should marry before the youngest. In short, their father, named Laban, forced Jacob to marry Leah; and then, with Rachel. Jacob had no choice but to accept Laban's imposition because he was deeply in love with Rachel. Later, Jacob married Rachel. Leah felt Jacob's rejection, but her faith in God helped her endure that sad situation (Genesis 27:41-45; 28:1-4; 29:1-35; 30:9-24; 31:1-55).

We continue with Zipporah, the eldest of seven daughters of a priest of Midian, named Jethro. After a series of incidents in Moses' life, Zipporah became his wife. Zipporah and Moses had several sons, and they lived in Midian. But on a normal day of grazing, Moses saw a bush burning in fire and not being consumed. At that very moment, Moses received God's call to deliver the Hebrew people from slavery in Egypt. However, when Moses was on his way with his family to Egypt to fulfill his mission, the Lord decided to kill Moses for postponing the circumcision of his son Eleazar. It was Zipporah who saved Moses from death.

Zipporah took a sharp flint, put it on her son's foreskin, and seizing her husband's genitals, exclaimed:

"*You are my blood husband.*"

Immediately, God spared Moses' life (Exodus 2. 3. 4. 5).

We continue with a woman of great spiritual and historical significance. Revered and admired by all Christians for the purity of their hearts and obedience to God. She is Mary or the Blessed Virgin Mary, mother of Jesus. A young woman with great faith in God and noble feelings. The angel Gabriel appeared to Mary and announced that she would conceive a child by the power and grace of the Holy Spirit. Her pure soul and faith in God enabled Mary to accept the words of the angel, to whom she replied:

"*Behold, I am the handmaid of the Lord, may your word be fulfilled in me.*"

The angel also informed Mary that he had visited Elizabeth, his relative, who was unable to conceive children. But God heard her pleas, and at the time, she was in the sixth month of pregnancy. After Mary heard the words of the angel Gabriel, this servant of the Lord decided to visit her relative Elizabeth. Indeed, Elizabeth was pregnant. When Mary arrived, and Elizabeth heard her greeting, she exclaimed:

"Blessed art thou among women, and blessed is the fruit of thy womb."

(Luke 1:8; 38-56; 2:1-52; Matthew 1:18-25; 2:7-11; 16-23).

Another biblical argument quotes Deborah and Jael. Deborah was a Jewish prophetess, and the only female judge in Israel. Both women stand out due to a conflict between Jews and Canaanites. That scenario points to General Barak, who belongs to Israel's army. This commander had to confront the commander of King Jabin of Canaan's troops. This is what God had ordained and transmitted through the prophetess Deborah, who was exercising her functions as Israel's magistrate. This prophetess gave moral support to General Barak to lead the Jewish army. General Barack himself even asked Deborah to accompany him during that campaign. Deborah's faith in God, her spiritual strength and security, were decisive in instilling in General Barack confidence in God and self-assurance in him in the face of the enemy forces of Commander Sisera of Canaan.

On the other hand, Jael was a woman who did not belong to the Israelite people, but she took their side. Jael took advantage of the tiredness of the Canaanite commander Sisera, and killed him. For this reason, General Barack won the battle against the Canaanites. Both women, Deborah and Jael, played a pivotal role in that victory. Religious beliefs based on faith in God were the spiritual foundations that, in cases such as the one mentioned above, motivated many of these biblical women to act defensively against their adversaries, in order to favor their community. The case of Deborah and Jael is a historical event of great relevance to the Hebrew people (Judges 4:4-23; Genesis 35:6-8).

At another point, a woman with a brave spirit, Abigail, appears. She defended her family from the wrath of David and his army. It happened when David was at war with King Saul, and he asked Abigail's husband, a very wealthy man named Nabal, for money to meet the expenses of his battle. But Nabal adamantly refused to cooperate in his political causes. This made David very angry, and he decided to go to Nabal's house to collect the offense from him. Fortunately, Abigail intervened. She went to meet David, who was approaching her house with a battalion of armed and furious men. Abigail brought them provisions; At the same time, she pleaded with David not to shed innocent blood because of her husband's recklessness (1 Samuel 25:10-12, 22). David listened to her words, accepted her help, and returned to his military camp.

Many valuable women are contemplated in the Holy Bible. Each of them was guided by their faith, kindness, love, courage, or determination. In this sense, it is worth presenting Esther, also known as Queen Esther, for having been chosen as the wife of King Ahasuerus of Persia. During her reign, this virtuous woman learned of an evil plan by Aman, the king's prime minister, to murder all of her fellow Jews living in that Persian empire. Immediately, Queen Esther set out to intervene on behalf of her people. After this queen flattered the king by offering him several banquets in his honor, she informed him of the iniquitous plan of her prime minister.

The king loved Esther; For that reason, he drew up another decree that allowed the Jews to defend themselves against all aggression against them. But the most significant thing about Esther was the note of faith she sent to the Jewish population. It was a devotional message, of trust in God. Queen Esther told the Israelites to "stay three days in fasting and prayer." In the letter, she also told them that she would do the same. It was a matter of first seeking the support of the Almighty, God the Father, to achieve triumph in such a difficult situation. The Jews were victorious thanks to the intervention of Queen Esther, and the support of King Ahasuerus. The story of Queen Esther is one of the most laudable in Jewish tradition (Esther 3:13-15; 4:1. 5).

Just as the Bible quotes many virtuous women; it also presents others who did not show morality or obedience to God. On this subject, it is appropriate to introduce Lot's Wife. His name does not appear in the Bible because the important person for our Father God was Lot, who was a man of faith. Lot was righteous and kind, so the Lord loved him. Therefore, God sent two angels to warn Lot to leave the city of Sodom where he lived with his family, because it would be destroyed. However, the angels told Lot that, during his emigration, he and his family had to fulfill a condition. It came down to this: leaving the city, none of them could look back, under any circumstances.

Despite the angels' warning, Lot's wife was curious. She wanted to see what was happening in that city, and she looked back. Instantly, Lot's wife turned into a pillar of salt. That is one of the punishments provided to themselves by those who disobey our eternal Father,

12

God. This entire passage is documented in the Bible (Genesis 18; 19:1-38).

Other meritorious women are the prophetesses: The prophetess Mary or Miriam, sister of Moses and Aaron. His presence was instrumental in the Hebrew Exodus. The prophetess Anna; he was present at the presentation of Jesus in the Temple in Jerusalem. Prophetess Huldah interceded with the Lord on behalf of King Josiah. On the other hand, we individually present other biblical women, such as: Princess Henutmire, Moses' foster mother. Rebekah, wife of Isaac; the son of the patriarch Abraham. Mary Magdalene, disciple of Jesus.

In the same way, we show the life of Ruth, a Moabite woman who left her people to serve God. Also, the Shulamite, a beautiful young protagonist of the book: "Song of Songs". Then there is Susanna, a beautiful young woman who was the victim of the wickedness of two old men. Likewise, Priscilla was a Christian woman who acted alongside her husband Aquila, both friends of Paul of Tarsus. We continue with two sisters who are very precious to our Lord Jesus Christ: Martha and Mary, sisters of Lazarus.

Another Gospel episode brings us to the Samaritan woman, to whom Jesus asked for water from a well built by Jacob. On the other hand, a famous event involves Judith, a biblical heroine who saved the inhabitants of Bethulia from the general Holofernes, who was acting under the orders of King Nebuchadnezzar II. The women mentioned above are just a few of the many who have been mentioned in the different chapters of the books contained in the Bible.

The purpose of this book is to convey a Christian message of faith and love for God the Father to all readers. Especially, to all women globally. In fact, the stories of each of the female biblical figures presented in this Christian collection can help us enormously to achieve that purpose. The writer's deep desire is to empower every woman on earth with faith; in this way, all the homes of the world will be under the grace of our Creator, God. Indeed, when we act according to Christ's commandments, we receive from Him many blessings, which are manifested in our families and ourselves.

Otherwise, our bad deeds could drag us into despairing abysses where all kinds of misfortune prevail; such as misfortunes, illnesses, and deaths.

Emphasizing, women are the pillars of our homes. Therefore, when we lean on our wonderful Lord, God and Father, our homes become little paradises on this planet Earth.

Sisters, if there is a lack of faith in us women, it could lead us not to give the deserved importance to the religion and morals that we need so much, and at the same time, favor our families. Since religious concepts and good behaviors act in our favor, enriching our loved ones with health, love and peace.

When we act contrary to religious teachings, we not only destroy ourselves, we also cause enormous harm to our innocent children. Moreover, the catastrophic effects of our skepticism toward the religious aspect could go beyond our familiar environment by linking other human beings. If that were the case, we would cause greater damage. Let us choose the best path, that of perfect good, which we can only attain when we are in direct contact with our exalted holy Father, God.

*I conclude the introduction to this Bible collection, **The Women** of the Bible, with a phrase from our Lord Jesus Christ, which can have a positive effect on us of increasing faith in the Lord. Also, the content of these holy words of our Lord Jesus Christ can help us to improve our actions; since they make us happy or unhappy beings. Blessed and protected by our holy Father or ruined, failed and unhappy, because of the lack of protection that our Lord gives to His true children. The Gospel of Luke, in chapter 11, verse 13, says the following:*

"If you, being evil, know how to give good things to your children,

How much more will the Father in heaven give the Holy Spirit to those who are Him!

Ask! ".

(Luke 11:13).

In the Gospel of Matthew, Jesus says:

"By their fruits you will know them.

Perhaps grapes are gathered from thorns, or

figs from thistles.

Every good tree bears good fruit, but a bad

tree bears bad fruit. "

(Matthew 7:16-17).

Preface

This edition, entitled Women Visited by the Angel Gabriel refers to: The Blessed Virgin Mary and Elizabeth, is an essential part of the collection of biblical books, The Women of the Bible. This is Mary, mother of our Lord Jesus Christ; and Elizabeth, his relative. Both were visited by the archangel Gabriel to bless their pregnancies. Therefore, Elizabeth conceived her son John in her old age. Meanwhile, Mary, a pure young woman, was chosen by the Lord to be the mother of our Savior Jesus Christ; A wonderful being who changed the lives and stories of all humans.

When Mary was visited by the angel Gabriel, she was a young virgin, humble and obedient who faithfully obeyed the laws of the Most High, the creator of all that exists. Mary was of Jewish origin, from the city of Nazareth in Galilee. She was the daughter of Jehoiachin and Anna, both descendants of King David. The name Maria or Mariam means: "Drop of the Sea" or "Star". According to the Gospels of Luke and Matthew, as well as the book of Acts of the Apostles, Mary lived in the late 1st century BC. A.D., and until the middle of the 1st century A.D. C.

At the time of the appearance of the angel Gabriel, Mary was Joseph's betrothed; a man belonging to the lineage of David. One day, Mary was at home when she was unexpectedly visited by an angel. It was the angel Gabriel who greeted her as follows:

"Hail, much favored!

The Lord is with thee; blessed are thou among women. "

(Luke 1:28).

The Gospel according to Luke says that when Mary heard the angel's words, she did not know what to answer. This maiden was totally surprised. Mary's embarrassment was perceptible. So the angel perceived him and said to him,

"Mary, do not be afraid, for you have found favor with God.

Now you will conceive in your womb and give birth to a son,

and you shall call his name JESUS. This one will be big,

and he shall be called the Son of the Most High; and the Lord God will give him the throne of

David, his father; and he shall reign over the house of Jacob forever,

and his kingdom will have no end."

(Luke 1:30-33).

Mary was only betrothed to Joseph, they had not yet married. Therefore, she asked the angel how that would happen because she had not been touched by some man. The angel Gabriel's response follows:

"The Holy Spirit will come upon you, and the power of the Most

High will overshadow you; wherefore also the Holy Being who

shall be born shall be called the Son of God. And behold, thy

kinswoman Elizabeth, she also hath conceived a son in her old age; and this is the sixth month for her, whom they called barren; for nothing is impossible with God."

(Luke 1:35-37).

Mary was a young woman of faith. She believed and accepted the words of the angel who acted as a messenger of the Lord, God the Father. Sure enough, Mary replied to the angel Gabriel:

"Behold, I am the handmaid of the Lord; let it be done to me according to your word. "

(Luke 1:38).

Mary was shocked by the arrival of the angel Gabriel, and his words. She didn't know about her relative Elizabeth's pregnancy until the angel told her. So Mary decided to visit Elizabeth, who lived on a hill in Hebron, Judea. Elizabeth was married to Zechariah, a priest of the line of Abijah. Both were advanced and very religious. They had not had children because Elizabeth was barren. However, the angel Gabriel visited them six months before showing up at Mary's house. In response, Elizabeth became pregnant in her old age, thanks to the Lord's mercy (Luke 1:5-8).

Mary came to the house of Zechariah and Elizabeth. As she stood at the door of his house, he saluted. As soon as Elizabeth heard his greeting, the child leaped into her womb and she was filled with the

Holy Spirit. Because of her great emotion, Elizabeth exclaimed in a loud voice:

"Blessed are you among women, and blessed is the fruit of your womb.

Who am I that the mother of my Lord should visit me?

Look, as soon as your greeting reached my ears, the child jumped for joy in my belly. Blessed are you who believed!

For what the Lord has told you will be fulfilled. "

(Luke 1:39-45).

John and Jesus were born and raised. There was a six-month age difference between them. First John was born, and then Jesus. Each one came into the world to carry out an evangelizing mission of spiritual salvation of the souls of all humans. As John announced the coming of the Savior Jesus Christ, and baptized in His name; Jesus was spiritually preparing to begin his divine ministry. But first, Jesus was baptized by John. At the moment of His baptism, He received the Holy Spirit that His Father God sent Him from on high.

Christ Jesus said,

"He who is not born again of water and the spirit cannot see the kingdom of God."

(John 3:3).

That was the mission of John the Baptist, son of Elizabeth and Zechariah, to prepare the way for our Savior Jesus. Because God the Father's plans are perfect. The Almighty granted Elizabeth the grace to conceive her son John to herald the arrival of the long-awaited Messiah, her beloved son. Speaking of Jesus' ministry, John the Baptist said, **"He is the Lamb of God who takes away the sins of the world."**

Mary was the mother of the greatest man born on this planet Earth, Jesus. It was He who, with His great love, divided time and human history in two. Christ is the Savior of mankind. The whole Christian faith is concentrated in its great universal power. Because of his high spiritual level, he was consecrated and legitimized as the Only Begotten and Beloved of God. Their ministry is based on love, mercy, peace, humility, justice, and service.

His mercy has been the source of inspiration for millions of Christian hearts. Basically, those who seek to create a covenant with their Savior Jesus Christ, through the Holy Scriptures. The faith of all its faithful has reached more than half of humanity through all religious temples, with a presence in the most important countries of the world.

Jesus was a man of humble heart, without academic degrees; but endowed with a sublime Perfection, that is why he completely changed the life and history of all the inhabitants of this planet. Through His Ministry, Christ brought us out of darkness to show us through the light of His Being that there is a clear and luminous path that can lead us to the Kingdom of God.

Our Lord Jesus Christ said:

"I am the light of the world; The one who follows me,

He will not walk in darkness,

but he will have the light of life."

(John 8:12).

The Virgin Mary, Mother of Jesus Christ

The Women of the Bible

The Virgin Mary

Mary was a young virgin of Jewish origin, from the city of Nazareth in Galilee. She was the daughter of Jehoiachin and Anna, both descendants of King David. According to the Gospel of Luke, the Gospel of Matthew, and the Acts of the Apostles, Mary lived in the late 1st century BC. A.D., and until the middle of the 1st century A.D. The Qur'an also affirms this fact (7th century). In another context, Islam's Holy Book acknowledges that Mary was the mother of Jesus, but mentions her by her Aramaic and Arabic name, Mariam. The name Mariam means:

"Drop of the Sea " or "Starfish ".

The evangelist Matthew says of Mary that she is the woman to whom the prophet Isaiah referred when he said:

"Therefore the Lord himself will give you a sign: Behold, the Virgin will conceive and give birth to a son, and they will name him Emmanuel; Translated it means: God with us. "

(Isaiah 7:14; Luke 1:35).

24

The presence of the Blessed Virgin Mary is legitimized by the main currents of early Christianity (1st, 2nd, 3rd and early 4th centuries), and made up the biblical Canon. The early period ended at the Council of Nicaea in 325 AD. It was the first council of the Catholic Church. This congress took place while the twelve apostles of Jesus were still alive.

The Blessed Virgin Mary was not only the mother of our Savior Jesus, the Messiah, sent by our Lord, the Eternal Father; Our Lady was also an eyewitness to his painful crucifixion. After the passion and death of our Lord Jesus Christ, the Virgin Mary formed the first Christian praying community. Before the coming of the Holy Spirit, the great day of Pentecost took place.

The Catholic and Orthodox Churches attribute to the Virgin Mary the faculties of intercessory before her Son Jesus Christ. Starting from the Gospel of John about his intervention at the "Wedding at Cana", where Jesus turned water into wine. The Virgin Mary is identified as the mother of God. A term ascribed to her at the Council of Ephesus, A.D. 431. C.

In the same way, the Virgin Mary is called "Blessed" after the text of the Gospel of St. Luke (Luke 1:39-45), which comes from the annunciation of the angel Gabriel. This expression is also written in the "Magnificat" of the Virgin Mary.

The Annunciation

Mary was Joseph's fiancée, belonging to the lineage of David. One day, Mary was at home when she was unexpectedly visited by an angel. It was the angel Gabriel who greeted her as follows:

"Hail, much favored! The Lord is with you; blessed are you among women."

(Luke 1:28).

The Gospel according to Luke says that Mary, when she heard these words, did not know what to answer; She was totally shocked. Mary's embarrassment was perceptible. So the angel said to him,

"Mary, do not be afraid, for you have found grace before God.

Now you will conceive in your womb and give birth to a son,

and you shall call his name Jesus. This one will be big,

and he shall be called the Son of the Most High;

and the Lord God will give him the throne of

David, his father; and he shall reign over the

house of Jacob

Forever

and his kingdom will have no end."

(Luke 1:30-33).

Mary was only betrothed to Joseph, they had not yet married. Therefore, she said to the angel how that would happen because she had not been touched by some man. These were Mary's words:

"How can this happen, since I don't know a

man?"

The angel Gabriel's response follows:

"The Holy Spirit will come upon you, and the

power of the Most High will overshadow you;

wherefore also the Holy Being who shall be born

shall be called the Son of God.

And behold, thy kinswoman Elizabeth, she also

hath conceived a son in her old age;

and this is the sixth month for her, whom they

called barren;

for nothing is impossible with God. "

(Luke 1:35-37).

Mary was a young woman of faith, worthy, obedient and humble. She believed and accepted the words of the angel who acted as the Lord's messenger. Accordingly, Mary replied to the angel Gabriel:

"Behold, I am the handmaid of the Lord;

let it be done to me according to your word. "

(Luke 1:38).

Mary in the house of Zechariah and Elizabeth

Mary was shocked by the arrival of the angel Gabriel, and his words. She didn't know about her relative Elizabeth's pregnancy until the angel told her. So Mary decided to visit Elizabeth, who lived on a hill in Hebron, Judea. Elizabeth was married to Zechariah, a priest of the line of Abijah. Both were advanced and very religious. They had not had children because Elizabeth was barren. However, the angel Gabriel visited them six months before showing up at Mary's house. Indeed, Elizabeth became pregnant in her old age, thanks to the Lord's mercy (Luke 1:5-8).

Mary came to the house of Zechariah and Elizabeth, and standing at the door of their house, she greeted them. When Elizabeth heard his greeting, the child leaped in her womb and was filled with the Holy Spirit. Because of her great emotion, Elizabeth exclaimed in a loud voice:

"Blessed are you among women, and blessed is the fruit of your womb.

Who am I that the mother of my Lord should visit me?

Look, as soon as your greeting reached my ears,

the child jumped for joy in my belly.

Blessed are you who believed!

For what the Lord has told you will be fulfilled. "

(Luke 1:39-45).

Obviously, the angel Gabriel informed Elizabeth of Mary's pregnancy. He also told him about the greatness of Jesus. Otherwise Elizabeth would not have said to Mary the following words: "Who am I that the mother of my Lord should visit me?" Even Elizabeth's last sentences have a meaning: "Blessed are you who believed! For what the Lord has told you will be fulfilled. "

Elizabeth spoke these words to Mary, because it happened, just before Elizabeth conceived her son, that an angel appeared to Zechariah, her husband, announcing Elizabeth's pregnancy. The biblical text does not mention the name of the angel, it could have been Gabriel himself. The matter is this: Sachariah did not believe in the angel, because Elizabeth was of advanced age. Because of his unbelief, Sachariah was dumb, and spoke after his son was born (Luke 1:10-19).

Mary and Elizabeth

Below is the verse Mary said to Elizabeth called:

"The Magnificat "

"My soul magnifies the Lord;

And my spirit rejoices in God

my Savior.

For he has beheld the lowliness of his servant; For

behold, henceforth all generations shall call me

blessed.

For the Mighty One has done great things for

me; Holy is his name.

And his mercy is from generation to generation

to those who fear him.

He did feats with his arm; He scattered the proud

in the thoughts of their hearts.

He removed the mighty from their thrones, and

exalted the lowly.

He filled the hungry with good things, and sent the

rich empty.

He helped his servant Israel, remembering

mercy

Of which he spoke to our fathers,

To Abraham and his descendants forever".

Mary stayed at Zechariah and Elizabeth's house for about three months, then returned home.

(Luke 1:46-56).

The Angel of the Lord appeared to Joseph while he slept

The angel spoke to Joseph

The Gospel of Matthew and Luke explain the reaction of Joseph, Mary's betrothed, to learning that she had conceived without him having touched her. Joseph was an honorable and righteous man. Despite her disappointment, he didn't want to defame her. Therefore, Joseph thought to discreetly distance himself from Mary. But the Lord sent an angel to speak with Joseph while he slept. In his dreams, the angel said to Joseph:

"Joseph, son of David, do not be afraid to receive Mary your wife, for that which is conceived in her is of the Holy Spirit.

She will give birth to a son, and you shall call him Jesus, for he will save his people from their sins".

When Joseph awoke, he did everything as the angel of the Lord had told him. Joseph received Mary; but he did not touch her until after she gave birth to Jesus (Matthew 1:18-25).

At that time, Emperor Augustus Caesar issued an edict announcing a nationwide census. It said that everyone had to be registered. Therefore, people who were living in or visiting other cities had to return to their place of birth. Definitely, Joseph had to leave for his *hometown, Bethlehem, to be counted. At the time, Mary was pregnant with Jesus.*

Joseph and Mary were to set out from Galilee in Nazareth to Bethlehem in Judea. When they arrived in that city, Mary was presented with childbirth. However, the inn there was full due to the census, and they couldn't find another place to stay.

Birth of the Child Jesus

Upon arriving in Bethlehem, the only inn there was full due to the census ordered by Emperor Augustus Caesar. Consequently, they were forced to stay in a stable, and there Mary gave birth to the baby Jesus. Afterward, Mary covered him with swaddling clothes, and laid him down in the manger (Luke 2:1-7). The Evangelist Luke recounts, in detail, all this sacred and historical revelation that encompasses the Christian world. The birth of our Lord Jesus Christ is an event recognized by most religions, globally, as a true event of great spiritual significance.

His glorified birth was the greatest event in the history of humanity, because that child is the Son of God who became man and gave us his divine ministry, gave his life, dying on the cross, for the salvation of our souls. His name is Jesus, of Aramaic origin, and in this language he is Yeshua. The meaning of Jesus is "God Saves" or "Savior." Concerning this sacred name, St. Bernardine of Siena expressed the following:

"This is the Most Holy name longed for by the

patriarchs, eagerly awaited,

sued with groans,

Invoked with sighs,

required with tears, given at the arrival of the

fullness of grace".

Adoration of the Shepherds of the Child Jesus

According to the evangelist Luke, on the night of Jesus' birth there were shepherds in that region who were on vigil tending their flocks. An angel of the Most High came to them and said to them,

"The glory of the Lord has surrounded them with brightness".

Understandably, these pastors were afraid. The angel sensed their fears, and said to them:

"Do not be afraid; For behold, I bring you tidings of great joy, which shall be to all the people: for unto you is born unto you this day in the city of David a Saviour, who is Christ the Lord.

This will serve as a sign to you:

You will find the babe wrapped in swaddling clothes, lying in a manger".

The Evangelist Luke relates that a multitude of heavenly hosts also appeared to them praising God and proclaiming:

"'Glory to God in the highest, and

On earth peace and goodwill for men!".

(Luke 2:8-14).

The Virgin Mary and the Child Jesus
(From the Evangelist, Luke)

Circumcision and Purification of Jesus

Jesus was circumcised eight days after his birth. It was at that moment that the child was given the name JESUS, which the angel Gabriel had proposed to Mary when he presented himself to her, before the child was conceived. Soon the time of purification was fulfilled, according to the law of Moses. From what is written in the law of the Lord, which says:

"Every male who opens the womb shall be called holy to the Lord".

According to the same law, Jesus' parents were to offer a pair of turtledoves or two moths for the act of purification. Under that law, Joseph and Mary took the child to Jerusalem to be presented to the Lord. (Luke 2:21-24).

At that time there lived in Jerusalem a pious and righteous man who was waiting for the consolation of Israel, his name was Simeon. The Holy Spirit had revealed to him that he would not die without seeing the Lord's Anointed. The Bible says that Simeon, moved by the Holy Spirit, went to the Temple in Jerusalem on the same day that Jesus' parents brought him to their presentation. When Simeon saw the child, he took him in his arms and blessed God (Luke 2:25-28).

Simeon exclaimed:

"Now, Lord, send your servant away in peace,

According to your word;

For my eyes have seen your salvation,

Which thou hast prepared in the presence of all peoples;

Light for revelation to the Gentiles,

And the glory of your people Israel".

(Luke 2:29-32).

After pronouncing these words, Simeon blessed the child Jesus, and turning to Mary said:

"Behold, this man is appointed for the fall and for the rising of many in Israel, and for a sign that it shall be contradicted, and you yourself shall pierce your soul with a sword. in order to expose the intentions of many hearts".

(Luke 2:33-35).

Anna the Prophetess was also there. She was the daughter of Phanuel, of the tribe of Asher. She was an elderly lady, a widow, and she did not leave the temple. He was, night and day, serving in the sanctuary with fasts and prayers. She went to Joseph, Mary, the baby Jesus, and Simeon, and when she saw Jesus she gave thanks to God. He spoke of the child to all believers who were waiting for Israel's redemption. Jesus grew, and so did His wisdom and God's grace (Luke 2:36-40).

El Niño Jesús en el Templo de Jerusalén

Hablando con los doctores de la Ley Mosaica
William Brassey Hole
(1915-1917)

Jesus meeting with the doctors of the Law in the Temple of Jerusalem

Every year, Joseph and Mary went to Jerusalem for the Passover Feast. When Jesus was twelve years old, his parents took him to that feast, according to the custom of the feast. When he returned, the baby Jesus stayed in Jerusalem. No one noticed his absence; nor his parents, Joseph and Mary. They went with relatives, friends and acquaintances. Therefore, they thought Jesus was among them. After walking a full day, his parents missed him, and they started looking for him.

Not finding him among the members of the caravan, Joseph and Mary returned to Jerusalem. Three days passed, looking for him everywhere. Finally, they went to the temple in Jerusalem. There, Jesus was in the midst of the doctors of the Law, who listened to him and asked him questions. Because of Jesus' answers, everyone was amazed at his intelligence and his answers. for He was only a child (Luke 2:41-47). This was his first sublime note that showed his Divine gifts as the Son of the Highest Lord.

When Joseph and Mary saw the baby Jesus, Mary's uneasiness was immediately revealed, and she said to him:

"Why have you done this to us? Your father and I have searched for you in anguish".

Jesus answered:

"Why were you looking for me? Didn't you know that

Do I need to be in my Father's business?".

However, his parents did not understand his words, and returned to Nazareth where they lived. The Holy Bible says,

"Mary kept all those things in her heart.

Whereas,

Jesus grew in wisdom, stature, and grace, toward God and man".

(Luke 2:48-52).

Adoration of the Three Wise Men to the Child Jesus

The Three Wise Men

We saw the evangelist Luke's account of the birth of Jesus. While this apostle mentions the visit of shepherds to Jesus' manger; In that same historic event, the evangelist Matthew depicts the arrival of the "Three Kings." In his Gospel, St. Matthew describes the arrival of wise men who came from the east to Bethlehem in Judea to meet the baby Jesus. The Three Wise Men asked:

"Where is the king of the Jews, who has been born? For we have seen his star in the east, and we have come to worship him".

The words of the wise men disturbed King Herod and all who heard them in Jerusalem. That resulted in a summons of Herod with the chief priests and scribes of the city. Herod's purpose was to inquire into the proper birthplace of Jesus Christ. They all agreed that it would be in Bethlehem of Judea; for so foretold by the prophet Micah:

"And you, Bethlehem, from the land of Judah, You are not the least among the princes of Judah;

For out of thee shall come a guide,

Who will feed my people Israel".

(Micah 5:2; Matthew 2:1-6).

After Herod's important meeting with the chief priests and scribes of the city, he spoke secretly with the magi. He told them to go to Bethlehem, and if they found the child to tell him because he too would go to worship him. The wise men departed and were guided by the same star that they had seen in the east. Then the star stopped at the place where Joseph and Mary were with the baby Jesus.

Before entering the place, the magicians felt immense joy. Entering, they saw Mary with the child. Then the Magi prostrated themselves before the baby Jesus, worshipped him, and offered him some gifts that they had selected for him. Among the gifts were gold, frankincense and myrrh. All present were amazed at the words of the magi; but Mary remained silent, keeping all these things in her heart (Matthew 2:7-11).

The Blessed Virgin Mary and the Child Jesus in Egypt

Flight to Egypt

The Lord protected the infant Jesus from Herod's wrath. While Joseph was sleeping, an angel of the Lord came to him in a dream and said to him:

"Arise and take the child and his mother, and flee to Egypt, and stay there until I tell you; for it shall come to pass that Herod shall seek the child to kill him".

Joseph awoke, and quickly took the child and Mary, and they went out to Egypt. They remained there until Herod's death. In this way, what was foretold by the prophet Hosea was fulfilled, when he said:

"Out of Egypt I called my son".

(Hosea 11:1; Matthew 2:13-15).

Herod's fury was due to the contemptuous attitude of the wise men who did not return to the palace to see him and inform him of the child's location, as he had requested. The Magi went back to their own country taking another road; for it was revealed to them in a dream that they should not return to Herod. Starting from the premise left by the Magi, Herod felt mocked. Herod was very angry and ordered the execution of all children under two years of age in

Bethlehem and the communities adjacent to this city. (Matthew 2:16-17).

That fact confirmed what was foretold by the prophet Jeremiah, who said:

"A voice was heard in Ramah,

Great lamentation, weeping and groaning;

Rachel who mourns her children,

And she would not be comforted, because they perished".

(Jeremiah 31:15; Matthew 2:18).

Although many children died, nothing happened to the baby Jesus because the Lord protected him from Herod's wrath. After Herod died, the angel of the Lord appeared to Joseph in a dream, and revealed to him to return to Israel. The angel said to him:

"Arise, take the child and his mother, and go to the land of Israel, for those who sought the death of the child are dead".

So Joseph got up and took the child and his mother, and they came to the land of Israel. Then they went to the city of Nazareth in the region of Galilee. Here another prophecy was fulfilled, which announced that Christ would be called a Nazarene (Matthew 2:19-23).

Many prophets announced the coming of the Messiah. The prophet Isaiah said of his reign the following:

"*A rod will come out of the trunk of Jesse, and a*

branch will sprout from his roots.

And the Spirit of the Lord shall rest upon him;

spirit of wisdom and understanding,

Spirit of counsel and power,

spirit of knowledge and fear of the Lord.

And it will make him understand diligently in

the fear of the Lord.

He will not judge by the sight of his eyes, nor argue

by what his ears hear;

but he will judge the poor with justice, and argue
with equity for the meek of the earth;
and he shall smite the earth with the rod of his
mouth, and with the spirit of his lips he shall slay the
wicked.
And righteousness shall be the girdle of his loins,
and faithfulness the girdle of his girdle".

(Isaiah 11:1-5).

Transit of the Virgin Mary

The Catholic Church recognizes as the Transit or Dormition of the Virgin Mary, the glorification of her body through the definitive donation of her glorious immortality, without passing through death. It is the opposite of human death. The divine intervention of her Son Jesus Christ made it possible for her body and soul, already glorified, not to be separated in expectation of the Last Judgment; and ascend together into the Kingdom of Heaven.

Dormition of the Virgin Mary

Narrative of St. John Damascene on the Dormition of the Blessed Virgin Mary

St. John Damascene relates that, after the death of her beloved son Jesus, the Blessed Virgin Mary was, for about fourteen years, preaching the teachings of Jesus to the Jewish people. The Virgin Mary continued to help the sick and helpless. Comforting the dying and strengthening many sad or grieving people. However, the deep pain caused in the virgin by the crucifixion of her beloved Son Jesus Christ marked her, leaving in her being an immense desire to be reunited with Him. Therefore, after dedicating herself to the holy cause of her Son, the virgin felt the call to depart from this world.

The Virgin Mary warned the apostles, who loved her, that the date of her departure into eternity was approaching. Immediately, they prepared to travel to see her for the last time, and to receive from her holy lips her sacred blessing. The exalted mother of Christ Jesus spoke words of comfort and hope to each of them.

"Then, like one who falls asleep in the most placid of dreams.

She closed her eyes in a holy way, and her soul, a thousand times blessed, departed into eternity".

(St. John Damascene).

61

St. John Damascene indicated that the news of his death spread throughout the city. All the Christians came to his funeral. Rather, this one looked like an Easter procession. They all sang the hallelujah glorifying the Blessed Virgin. There were soft scents and soft music in the air. Meanwhile, the apostle Thomas did not make it in time to see the Virgin Mary or to be present at her tomb. With great sadness he said to the apostle Peter:

"You cannot deny me the great favor of being able to go to the grave of my most loving mother,

And give her one last kiss

to those holy hands that so often blessed me".

The apostle Peter agreed, and they all went to the holy sepulchre. They were near that place, when they began to smell very sweet aromas; and in the atmosphere, harmonious music in the air. When they arrived, they opened the tomb, but instead of the virgin's corpse, they found a large number of very beautiful flowers. On this great revelation, St. John Damascene:

"Jesus Christ had come, He had raised His Blessed Mother

and had taken her to heaven ".

This is what we call:

«The Assumption of the Virgin Mary».

St. John Damascene said:

"And which of us, if he had the powers of the Son of God,

Wouldn't he have done the same with his own Mother?".

St. John Damascene, Saint and Doctor of the Church, gives us the most reliable and beautiful account of the death of the Blessed Virgin Mary. Beautiful words of this saint to the Blessed Virgin Mary, below:

"The Mother of God did not die of illness,

because she did not have original sin and did not

have to receive the punishment of illness.

She did not die of old age, because she did not

have to grow old, since she did not receive the

punishment of the sin of her first parents: to grow

old, and to end up in weakness.

She died of love.

Such was the desire to go to heaven where her

Son was,

that this love made her die ".

(St. John Damascene).

Assumption of the Virgin Mary

Pope Pius XII proclaimed the Dogma of the Assumption of the Virgin Mary on November 1, 1950; He said:

"After praying to God many times and calling

upon the light of the Spirit of Truth, to the glory of

Almighty God,

who bestowed upon the Virgin Mary her peculiar

benevolence; for the honour of his Son,

immortal King of the ages and conqueror of sin

and death;

to increase the glory of the same august Mother,

and to the joy and gladness of the

whole Church,

by the authority of our Lord Jesus Christ, of the

Blessed Apostles Peter and Paul, and by our

own, we pronounce,

we declare and define it to be a divinely revealed

dogma of

the Immaculate Mother of God and ever-

Virgin Mary,

at the end of the course of her earthly life, was

assumed body and soul into the glory

of heaven".

(Pope Pius XII).

*The feast of the Assumption of the Blessed Virgin Mary is celebrated
every year on August 15.*

The Sepulchre of the Virgin Mary

According to the ancient ecclesiastical tradition of the Orthodox saints, the place dedicated to the burial of the Virgin Mary is located in the Church called: *The Sepulchre of the Virgin Mary*, located in the Kidron Valley, near Jerusalem. This church is located at the foot of the Mount of Olives, near the Basilica of Gethsemane. Today, this Church is Greek Orthodox and Armenian Apostolic. It allows the veneration of Orthodox-Copts, Syriac Orthodox, and Ethiopian-Orthodox.

In this Church of the Sepulchre of the Virgin Mary, are the tombs of her parents: Joachim and Anna, and her husband Joseph. The tombs can be reached via a steep staircase. Adjacent to the entrance of this Church is:

«The Grotto of the Tradition of the Catholics».

It was in this place that Jesus' arrest took place.

Prayers to the Blessed Virgin Mary

The Hail Mary:

"Hail Mary, full of grace, the Lord is with you. Blessed art thou among women, and blessed is the fruit of thy womb, Jesus.

Holy Mary, Mother of God, pray for us sinners, now and at the hour of our death".

Amen!

The Hail Mary is a traditional prayer of the Catholic Church, dedicated to the Virgin Mary, mother of Jesus Christ. The first part of this prayer has its biblical foundation in the Gospel according to Luke; Chapter 1, verse 43. The Hail Mary is the main prayer of the Angelus and the Rosary.

Hail Holy Queen:

"Hail, Queen and Mother of mercy, our life, our sweetness and our hope, God save you. We call you the banished sons of Eve,

To you we sigh, groaning and weeping in this vale of tears.

Come, then, Lady, our advocate, turn thy merciful eyes upon us, and, after this banishment,

Show us Jesus, the blessed fruit of your womb.

O clement, O pious, O ever-sweet Virgin Mary!

Pray for us, Holy Mother of God, that we may be worthy to attain the promise of God.

our Lord Jesus Christ".

Amen!

Note: *The Salve Regina, or La Salve, is one of the most well-known prayers in the Catholic Church. Originally, this prayer was written in Latin. First, the invocation was a major antiphon (verse or chant) and hymn. It is one of the four antiphons of the Breviary dedicated to the Blessed Virgin Mary.*

Blessed be your purity:

"Blessed be thy purity, and may it be eternally so, for a whole God delighteth in such a graceful beauty.

To you, heavenly princess, O holy virgin Mary,

I offer you on this day, soul, life and heart.

Look at me with compassion, don't leave me,

My Mother".

Amen!

The Regina Coeli:

"Rejoice, queen of heaven, hallelujah.

For the one you deserved to carry in your bosom, hallelujah.

He is risen, as he said, hallelujah.

Pray for us to God, hallelujah.

Rejoice and rejoice, Virgin Mary, hallelujah.

For the Lord is truly risen, hallelujah ".

Pray:

Oh, God! who, through the resurrection of your Son, our Lord Jesus Christ, have deigned to give joy to the world, grant that, through his Mother, the Virgin Mary, we may attain the joy of eternal life. By Christ our Lord Himself. Amen.

Note: This prayer, the Regina Coeli, replaces the recitation of the Angelus during the Easter season. The prayer is attributed to St. Gregory the Great.

Remember/Memorare:

"Remember, O most merciful Virgin Mary!

that it has never been heard of that any of those who

have come to your protection,

imploring your assistance and calling for your help,

has been forsaken.

Encouraged by this trust, I also turn to you,

O Mother, Virgin of virgins! ➤

and groaning under the weight of my sins, I dare

to appear before your sovereign presence.

O Mother of God, do not dismiss my

supplications, but listen to them and accept them

kindly".

Amen!

Note: *Acordaos or Memorare (in Latin), is a prayer to the Blessed Virgin Mary. Its first texts date back to the 15th century. The author of this beautiful prayer is unknown. It was attributed to St. Bernard of Clairvaux (1090-1153). Popularized by Claude Bernard the*

"Poor Priest" (1588-1641). In correspondence to such a lofty prayer, most popes grant partial indulgences to those who recite this prayer.

Catechesis:

What did we learn from the Virgin Mary?

Mary was a young virgin of pure feelings and much faith in the Lord, our eternal Father. Because of her blessed and honorable virtues, the Lord chose her to be the mother of our Savior Jesus Christ. In fact, it was not an ordinary human being, but the Christ; a being that the Jewish people have been waiting for for many years. His coming was foretold by several prophets, predecessors to Him. At the moment of her arrival in this world, the Lord sent the angel Gabriel to Mary's house to announce that she would become pregnant by the promised Messiah. The angel addressed her with the following words:

"Rejoice, full of grace!

The Lord is with thee; blessed art thou among women".

(Luke 1:26-28).

When the angel Gabriel spoke to Mary about her pregnancy, she humbly replied:

"Behold, I am the handmaid of

the Lord;

let it be done to me according to your word".

(Luke 1:38).

Mary, mother of Jesus Christ, was a highly blessed woman. She conceived Jesus through the power of the Holy Spirit. Jesus Christ was formed in her womb and the Virgin Mary raised him and watched him grow. What an enormous privilege of the ever-venerated Virgin Mary! We must all learn many things from the Virgin Mary; But the most important ones are listed below:

First: *Have full trust in the Lord.*

Second: *Respect His dispositions, because He is our God and heavenly Father, creator of all that exists, and works only for our good.*

Third: *To be servants of the Lord, like Mary, who humbly obeyed his plans.*

Eternal Blessings to the Mother of Christ, the Blessed Virgin Mary:

"Blessed art thou among women,

and blessed is the fruit of thy womb,

Christ Jesus".

Amen!

(Luke 1:39-45).

References:

- *(Luke 1:38).*

- *(Luke 1:5-8).*

- *(Luke 1:39-45).*

- *(Luke 1:10-19).*

- *(Luke 1:46-56).*

- *(Matthew 1:18-25).*

- *(Luke 2:1-7).*

- *(Luke 2:8-14).*

- *(Luke 2:21-24).*

- *(Luke 2:25-28).*

- *(Luke 2:29-32).*

- *(Luke 2:33-35).*

- *(Luke 2:36-40).*

- *(Luke 2:41-47).*

- *(Luke 2:48-52).*

- *(Micah 5:2; Matthew 2:1-6).*

- *(Matthew 2:7-11).*

- *(Matthew 2:16-17).*

- *(Hosea 11:1; Matthew 2:13-15).*

- *(Matthew 2:16-17).*

- *(Jeremiah 31:15; Matthew 2:18).*

- *(Matthew 2:19-23).*

- *(Pope Pius XII).*

- *(St. John Damascene).*

- *Council of Trent (Session VI, Canon 23).*

Feast of the Virgin Mary:

Since it is an event of the first order for the Christian faith, the celebration of Mary, mother of Christ, is a liturgical celebration with a degree of solemnity.

The dates below:

- *The Immemorial Roman Rite:*
  October 11.
- *The Reformation of the Roman Rite:*
  10 January; at the end of the Octave of Christmas.
- *The Ambrosian Rite of the Incarnation:*
  6th and last Sunday of Advent.
- *The Syriac and Byzantine Rites:*
  December 26.
- *The Coptic Rite (one of the Eastern liturgical rites of Christianity): January 16.*

The Catholic Church celebrates the coronation of the Virgin Mary, in the 5th Glorious Mystery of the Rosary.

Elizabeth, mother of John the Baptist

Image of Zechariah, Elizabeth, and Baby John
Zechariah writing the boy's name on a tablet

The Women of the Bible

Elizabeth

Elizabeth was one of the daughters of Aaron, brother of Moses, who delivered the Jews from slavery in Egypt. She was married to Zechariah, a priest of the line of Abijah. Both were very religious and of impeccable conduct; but they had no children because Elizabeth was barren. Luke's Gospel relates that one day, Zechariah was exercising the priesthood, and it was his turn to enter the sanctuary of the Lord to offer incense. All the people were outside praying and waiting for the hour of incense (Luke 1:5-9).

An Angel appeared to Zechariah

While Zechariah was inside the sanctuary, an angel of the Lord appeared to him. He was standing to the right of the altar. When Zechariah saw this, he was bewildered and frightened. But the angel said to him:

"Do not be afraid, for your prayer has been heard, and you

The woman Elizabeth will bear you a son whom you shall call John.

You 'll have joy and gladness,

and many shall rejoice at his birth, for he shall be

great before God.

He will not drink wine or drink, and he will be

full

of the Holy Spirit

even from his mother 's womb".

(Luke 1:10-15).

The angel went on to say:

"And many of the children of Israel will be

turned to the Lord their God,

and he shall go before him in the spirit and power of

Elijah,

To turn the hearts of parents to their children,

and the rebellious to the prudence of the righteous,

to prepare a people for the Lord

well disposed".

Then, Zechariah said to the angel:

"How will I know this?

Cause I'm old, and my wife

Elderly".

The angel answered:

"I am Gabriel, standing before God; and I have been sent to speak to you and give you this good news".

(Luke 1:16-19).

Zechariah's Unbelief

To Zechariah's unbelief, the angel Gabriel added:

"Now you will be dumb and you will not be able to speak until the day this is done,

because you did not believe my words, which will be fulfilled in due time".

During the time that Zechariah was talking with the angel Gabriel, the people outside waited impatiently for this priest to come out. But when he went out he could not speak to them, and he only did so through signs. All the believers supposed that he had seen some vision in the sanctuary. When Zechariah fulfilled the time of his ecclesiastical ministry, he went home. A few days later, Elizabeth conceived; but Zechariah shut himself up in his house for five months, and said:

"So has the Lord done to me in the days when he deigned to take away my reproach among men".

(Luke 1:20-25).

Birth of John the Baptist

At the end of her gestational period, Elizabeth gave birth to a boy. His relatives, friends, and neighbors were happy when they found out. On the eighth day they circumcised him, and called him after his father. but Elizabeth objected. She said, his name will be John. Then they asked Elizabeth, why? His name would be John if they didn't have anyone in the family with that name.

Quickly, they asked Zacarias, the boy's father. Then he asked for a tablet, and wrote:

"John is his name".

Suddenly, Zechariah began to speak blessing God. But his attitude caused fear among the neighbors, who wondered: "Who is this child?" Despite the conjectures of his relatives, friends, and neighbors, John grew up under the protection and grace of the Lord" (Luke 1:57-66).

Elizabeth, after the birth of John the Baptist

Zechariah's Prophecy

Zechariah, full of emotion, prophesied the following:

"Blessed be the Lord God of Israel,

Who has visited and redeemed his people,

And a mighty Savior raised us up

In the house of David his servant,

As He spoke by the mouth of His holy prophets

who were from the beginning;

Salvation from our enemies, and from the hand

of all who hated us;

To show mercy to our fathers,

And remember his holy covenant;

From the oath which he swore to Abraham our

father,

That he was to grant us

Who, delivered from our enemies,

Without fear we would serve you

In holiness and righteousness before him, all our

days.

And thou, child, prophet of the Highest Lord,

shall be called;

For thou shalt go before the presence of the Lord,

to prepare his ways;

To give knowledge of salvation to his people,

For the forgiveness of their sins,

By the tender mercy of our God,

With which the dawn visited us from on high,

To give light to those who dwell in darkness and in the shadow of death;

To set our feet on the path of peace.

And the child grew, and was strengthened in spirit: and he was in desolate places until the day of his appearing to Israel".

(Luke 1:67-80).

Elizabeth's joy was immense. The Lord had listened to His servants, Zechariah and Elizabeth, rewarding them with the arrival of a child, who not only filled their lives with blessing and happiness; His evangelizing doctrine also penetrated many hearts. His prophetic gifts went beyond the expectations of the people of that time. But John, the son of Elizabeth and Zechariah, baptized and announced the coming of the Messiah, Christ Jesus. He preached, and never claimed the privilege of being the Messiah.

When John preached, he said:

"After me comes one mightier than I, to whom I am not worthy to bow down and untie the strap of his shoes".

(Mark 1:7).

We call John the Baptist John for carrying out his evangelizing mission through baptism. John grew, and with him his love for the Lord. He dedicated himself to spreading the Holy Word of the Lord throughout Israel for the conversion of souls. John stayed on the path of faith; led by the Lord. He preached and baptized in the name of the Most High, the eternal Father. He was a forerunner of Jesus, whom he proclaimed, and then baptized himself. There were many who believed the words of John the Baptist.

(John 1:6-8; 7:19-23).

John the Baptist

Prophetic Passages

Here are some prophetic passages that confirm the presence of John the Baptist, messenger of the Lord:

"Behold, I am sending my messenger to prepare the way before me. Suddenly, the Lord they seek will enter the sanctuary; the messenger of the covenant that you so desire, see him come in, says the Lord".

(Malachi 3:1).

"And I will send you Elijah the prophet before the great and dreadful day of the Lord comes: he will reconcile fathers to sons, children to fathers, so that I will not come to destroy the earth".

(Malachi 3:23-24).

Isaiah's Prophecy:

"Look, I send ahead

to my messenger to prepare the way for you.

A voice cries out in the wilderness.

Prepare the way of the Lord.

Make straight their".

(Isaiah 40:3-5; Mark 1:3; Matthew 3:3; Luke 3:4).

Catechesis:

What did we learn from Elizabeth?

Elizabeth was one of the daughters of Aaron, brother of Moses, who freed the Jewish people from slavery in Egypt. She was the mother of John the Baptist, a relative of the Messiah, Jesus Christ. This noble woman spent many years asking the Lord for the grace to conceive a child. Elizabeth and Sacariah were honorable people. Both Elizabeth and her husband Zechariah followed the Lord's commandments. For their good conduct, both enjoyed a high reputation within their community.

The Bible relates that Zechariah was in the Temple in Jerusalem. when the archangel Gabriel came to visit him. This angel announced to him the coming of a son in his old age; Saying to him:

"Do not be afraid, Zechariah, for your request has been heard, your wife Elizabeth will bear you a son, whom you shall call John...".

(Luke 1:7-19).

However, Zechariah did not believe the angel Gabriel, not because of a lack of faith, but because of his advanced age and that of his wife Elizabeth.

Because of his unbelief Zechariah became mute, and spoke only after his son John the Baptist was born; and he respected the Lord's command, which was indicated by the angel Gabriel, by baptizing his son with the name of John. Elizabeth, on the other hand, was a woman of great faith in our Lord and God. This good and noble woman left us the following life lessons:

First: *Have absolute faith in the Lord, and keep His commandments:*

a) *The first one:* "Love God above all things and our neighbor as ourselves".

b) *The second one:* "Loving our neighbor as ourselves".

Second: *Persevere in our direct prayers to the Highest Lord, without hesitation. Patiently awaiting the accomplishment of the desired miracle; just as Elizabeth did, who never lost her faith in our wonderful and eternal Father God.*

Third: *Let us live with the full certainty that **the Lord** lives and does not forget us, but He waits for the ideal moment to give us what we long for. Let us imitate Elizabeth and succeed in our purposes by walking, side by side, with our holy Father, the Almighty.*

Proverb to the woman of faith in the Lord:

"Many women did good;

But you surpass them all".

Amen!

(Proverb 31:29).

St. Elizabeth
Church of San Saturnino

101

References:

- *(Luke 1:5-9).*
- *(Luke 1:10-15).*
- *(Luke 1:16-19).*
- *(Luke 1:20-25).*
- *(Luke 1:57-66).*
- *(Luke 1:67-80).*
- *(Mark 1:7).*
- *(John 1:6-8; 7:19-23).*
- *(Malachi 3:1).*
- *(Malachi 3:23'24).*
- *(Isaiah 40:3-5).*
- *(Mark 1:3).*
- *(Matthew 3:3).*
- *(Luke 3:4).*
- *(Proverb 31:29).*

Elizabeth's Feast

The Catholic Church considers Elizabeth a saint. His feast day is celebrated every year on November 5th. It is celebrated in the Anglican Church on September 5 each year, the same day as Zechariah's celebration. Meanwhile, the Lutheran Church considers Elizabeth a matriarch, and Zecharah a prophet. In this church his feast day is November 5th.

Made in the USA
Columbia, SC
30 November 2024

48023160R00057